SOMEONE TO LOVE

THE STORY OF CREATION

By Marilyn Lashbrook

Illustrated by Stephanie McFetridge Britt

**CANDLE
BOOKS**

The story of Creation provides wonderful opportunities for your child to learn about God's world. As you read this story, stop after the questions to allow your child to respond by pointing to the pictures. He will not only learn about God's world, he will also learn the deeper lesson behind the story — the lesson of God's love and power.

First published in the UK by Candle Books Ltd., 1993.
Reprinted 1994, 1996.
Distributed by SP Trust, Triangle Business Park,
Wendover Road, Aylesbury, Bucks HP22 5BL.

Co-edition arranged by Angus Hudson Ltd., London.

All enquiries to Angus Hudson Ltd., Concorde House, Grenville Place,
Mill Hill, London NW7 3SA, England.
Telephone: +44 181 959 3668
Fax: +44 181 959 3678

Printed in Hong Kong.

ISBN 0 948902 79 5

SOMEONE TO LOVE

THE STORY OF CREATION

By Marilyn Lashbrook

Illustrated by Stephanie McFetridge Britt

Taken from Genesis 1 and 2

Long, long ago, there was God.
But there were no people
for God to love.

No big people.
No little people.
Not even any
baby people.

And the world was a dark and empty place.

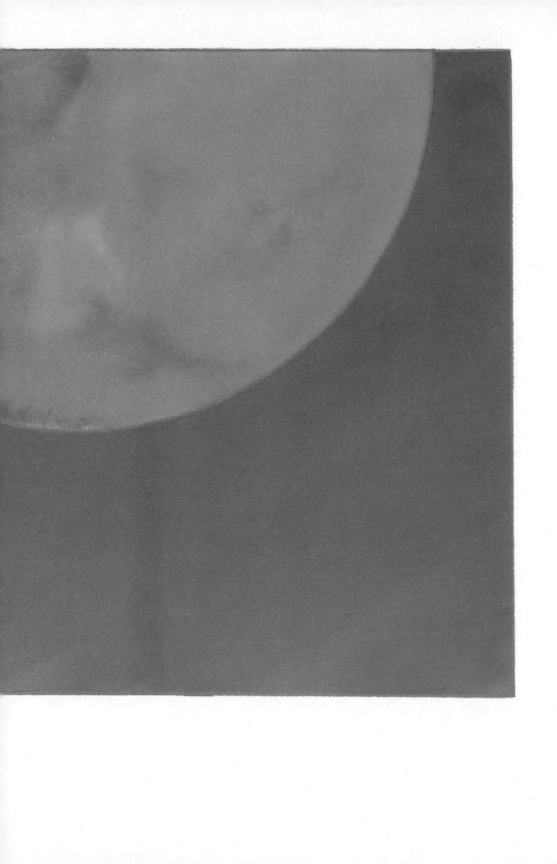

Then God said,
"Let there be light!"

And there was light.

And the light was good.

But there were still no people
for God to love.

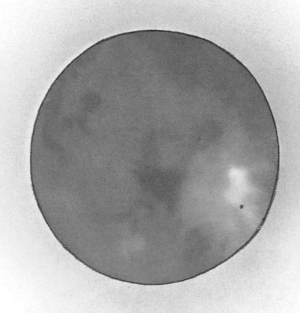

God made day.

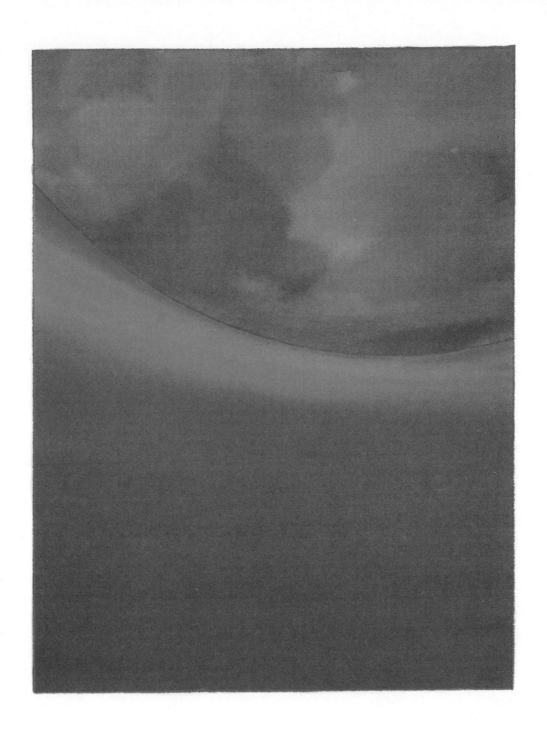

And He made night.

He made the beautiful blue sky.
And it was good.

But there were still no people
for God to love.

God moved the waters to one place
so there would be dry ground.

Then God made plants and trees.

Where is the apple tree?

Where is the orange tree?

Where are the strawberry plants?

Where are the banana trees?

God put the big, yellow sun
in the daytime sky.
He put twinkling stars and a glowing moon
in the night sky.

And the plants and trees
and sun and stars were all very good.
But there were still no people
for God to love.

Then, God made birds to fly in the sky.
Where is the red bird?
Where is the yellow bird?
Where is the blue bird?

God made fish to swim in the sea.
Do you see the big fish?
Do you see the little fish?

God made animals
to run and play in the green grass.

Can you count the animals?

God's world was no longer empty.
It was full of wonderful things.
But there were still no people
for God to love.

So God made a man and a woman.
God named the man Adam.

Adam named the woman Eve.

Now there were people for God to love.

And since that time,
God has loved all the big people,
and all the little people,

and all the baby people
who have ever lived
in His beautiful world.

ME TOO!
B O O K S

ME TOO!
R E A D E R S
